**For Carla Marie**

*My dearest friend,
closest confidante and muse.*

The Songwriter's Advocate
©2018 Matt Stinton

*All rights reserved.*
No part of this manuscript may be used or reproduced in any manner whatsoever without written permission from the publisher except in the case of brief quotations embodied in critical articles and reviews.

**Credits**
"Sea the Sea" ©2014 Matt Stinton
"One Thing Remains" ©2010 Bethel Music, Mercy/Vineyard Publishing/ChristaJoy Music Publishing
*TED Radio Hour*: "The Source of Creativity" ©2014 NPR

**FIRST EDITION**
*Printed in the United States with generous donations from family and friends through Kickstarter.com. Special thanks to John and Roxanne Pepe and team, John and Tiffany Matthews and team, and Matthew Spaier.*

Written and Produced by Matt Stinton
Portland, Maine USA
Edited by Lauren Stinton
Graphic Design by Amy Renée Miller

*instagram*: @mttstntn
mattstinton.com
mattandcarlastinton.com

# THE SONGWRITER'S
# ADVOCATE

*A Practical Guide
To Writing Stronger Songs*

MATT STINTON

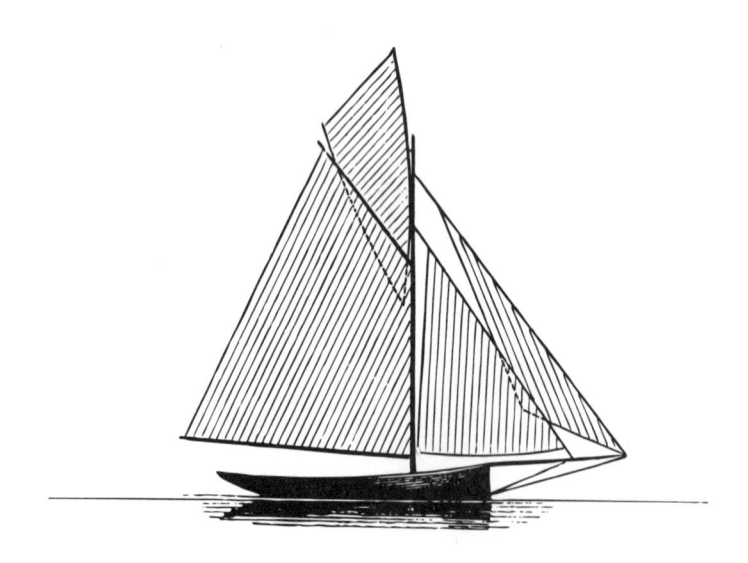

**Welcome to The Songwriter's Advocate.**

I began writing songs when I was six years old—swinging my legs and plunking away on the giant piano in our basement. While my first songs obviously weren't all that great, over the years I fell in love with the freedom I found in the process. It was a way to both express myself and create.

As I grew older, I began to learn about more of the day-to-day process of writing. About the frustrations of being stuck on an incomplete song and the sweet ecstasy of finally finishing it. Creating is a beautiful and, at times, painful process.

I firmly believe that songwriters are some of the most influential people in society. We are enamored with music creators because music has a way of moving us that no other art form can. With that realization should come a sense of responsibility, both to the listener who is being influenced by your words and to the One who planted the talent deep in the soil of your heart.

I wrote this guidebook in hopes that some of the things I've learned over the years will help you in your songwriting craft. While this book leans a little more toward writing corporate worship songs, the content is geared to help all songwriters. I hope it proves useful to you.

*Matt*

# PART ONE
# FINDING YOUR WAY

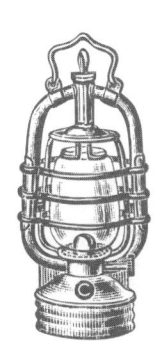

*"Inspiration is for amateurs. The rest of us just show up and get to work."*

Chuck Close

## BEFORE YOU EVEN START WRITING

Before we talk about the actual process of writing a song, I want to go over a few things first. I consider these to be foundational for any creative person because they need to be understood before you start creating. These are things I wish I had learned early on in my life. They would've saved me from a lot of headaches and wasted time and energy.

## EXERCISE

It is helpful to view creativity as a muscle. Like a muscle, it will never grow strong without being exercised. You've never seen a professional athlete who didn't train for game day. Drill after drill after drill. Nor have you ever seen a body builder bulk up without spending a tremendous amount of time in a gym.

Similarly, you have never heard of a great songwriter who didn't exercise their songwriting ability. Yes, there are some people who get lucky and write a hit song early on in their career, but that doesn't make them a great songwriter. It just means they wrote a great song once. To become a truly great songwriter, you have to write. Song after song after song.

I know this is very early in the book, but I'm going to go ahead and give you the best songwriting advice I have. Brace yourself because it's truly profound: **The more you write, the more you write.**

Once you've picked your jaw up off the floor, read on.

Too many of us tend to sit around and wait for inspiration to hit. We wait for "the spark" to come and save us from our writer's block. That, however, is not how great songwriters write. Great songwriters go looking for their inspiration instead of waiting for it to find them.

This guy who was an Olympic long-distance runner once visited my church. Even though the Olympics were months off at the time, he was running. A lot. If he was going to succeed in his sport, he needed to run all the time. He would have no chance of finishing a race if he just sat on his couch for months beforehand. He would be out of shape, and his body wouldn't be physically capable of performing the way he needed it to.

You're a smart person, so I'm sure you see where I'm going with this. To be a writer, you must be writing. You can't expect to write songs if you aren't writing.

## STARTING UP THE ENGINE

When you haven't been actively writing, you may find it difficult to get ideas the first few times you sit down to write. It's important to keep this in mind because a lot of people end up getting frustrated and want to throw in the towel. The truth of the matter is that writing when you haven't been is like trying to start a car engine in the middle of winter. While it takes a few turns to get started, the good news is once it's finally going, it runs better and better with each passing minute.

When you start writing after a period of idleness, either because your couch was really comfortable or because one of life's many challenges stole your energy, you have to realize it can be hard to write as if you've been writing the whole time. Like that engine in the cold, you have to give your creativity a few cranks before it starts to warm up.

This process is not as difficult as you might think. I've heard stories of people writing for hours every day, and that can sound quite intimidating, particularly for new writers or for people who don't have that amount of time available. I have found that consistency is just as important, if not more important, than the amount of time put into the process.

Not everyone will have a few hours every day to dedicate to writing, but I can guarantee that everyone has at least ten minutes. Consistently setting time aside, regardless of the length, helps keep the creative juices flowing. And as we all know, the more you write, the more you write.

## WRITE WHAT COMES EASILY TO YOU

I went through a dry spell of writing a few years back. I was focused on writing worship songs but wasn't actually able to write any. I put so much pressure on myself to keep up with my peers that I ended up shutting myself down completely. Finally, after a year or so of unsuccessful attempts, I decided to write the songs I actually had ideas for. And that's when I wrote my first EP, *See the Sea*.

The songs poured out of me. The creativity had been there all along, but I was trying to force it to be something specific instead of just letting it happen.

As writers, sometimes we feel pressure to produce something specific. The more we pressure ourselves, the less genuine our expression will be. While I'm an advocate for pushing yourself, you should never stop writing the songs that come easily. Craft them. Refine them. But don't despise them.

If you don't like what you're writing, that's okay. At least you're writing something. Everyone has to start somewhere. Even the most experienced songwriters don't write hits every time. Most people don't hear the half songs these writers never finished or the ones that didn't make the record. No one writes a hit every time, so go ahead and take that pressure off yourself.

## SELF-CRITICISM KILLS

Self-pressure and self-critique are the two most dangerous things for a songwriter.

I once listened to a podcast that featured a scientist named Charles Limb, who conducted a study on creativity. He wanted to know what happened inside the brain when people created. So he found a pianist who excelled in improvisation. This guy actually performed entire concerts off the cuff, meaning he made up the whole thing as he went along. He was a very creative person, to say the least. To best study the process of creativity, Limb needed to put the pianist in an MRI scanner. So he strapped a tiny keyboard to his knees, loaded him into a scanner and asked him to create. The results were fascinating.

The MRI let Limb monitor brain activity during the creative process. As the musician began to create and improvise, the parts of his brain that handle creativity and self-expression lit up on the screen. That makes sense, right? What stood out to me as I listened to this podcast was the discovery that the prefrontal cortex, which is believed to process self-monitoring, started shutting down.

Do you see the significance of that? While this was not the central point of the study, that fact stood out to me so clearly. The part of your brain that handles self-expression and the part of your brain that handles self-monitoring (a.k.a. self-awareness or self-consciousness) seem to be in competition. Expressing yourself creatively requires that your self-awareness and self-monitoring shut down.

I would argue that creativity and criticism cannot exist simultaneously. The more you second-guess and critique what you're doing, the harder it will be to create. When you're afraid of making a mistake, you cannot move forward confidently. Your brain is not actually wired to function that way. You will think yourself into a corner and wonder why it's so difficult to finish songs.

## SAY GOODBYE TO THE PERFECTIONIST

On occasion you may be able to write a song that conveys exactly what you want to say, but that will not happen all the time. You can't be a perfectionist if you're going to finish songs.

Perfectionism, at its heart, is criticism and we know how destructive that is to the creative process. It's driven by all the wrong motives. It's different than just trying to be a better writer. The urge to be a better writer comes from a desire to grow and to continually produce better and better songs. Perfectionism is based on fear of failure and of not being good enough in the eyes of others. It's about how you look and how you are perceived, not about becoming a better writer.

If you're a perfectionist, when it comes time to let someone listen to your song, any form of critique, even if it's constructive, will destroy you. It's far too easy to let the creation become a commentary on the creator. If this happens and someone criticizes your song, it means there's a problem with you.

You must remain teachable if you ever expect to grow, and perfectionism will keep that from happening.

## LEAVE COMPARISON AT THE DOOR

Everyone starts their songwriting journey at the same exact place: having not written a song before. In that regard, the playing field is even. However, if you know anything about trees, you know that not every tree grows at the same rate or to the same height or stature. Similarly, not every songwriter grows at the same rate or carries the same level of talent or anointing. That is a fact of life and it must be accepted. It doesn't make anyone more important than the next, but it does mean that one person's life and opportunities may look different than someone else's.

Comparison, like self-criticism, is a killer. Because everyone is at different points in their journey, one person will produce different results than the next. It is unfair to you to compare yourself with someone who is further along or, possibly, more gifted than you. Doing so will *always* result in frustration. You are not responsible to write songs like the next person. You are only responsible to steward what you have been given and to grow at your own pace.

It's incredibly important to understand this. We waste too much time when we compare ourselves with the person next to us. What we are actually doing in this process is idolizing the gifting of another while *undervaluing* what we have been given. This mindset is incredibly destructive and needs to be killed in our hearts.

## KNOW WHY YOU WRITE

You have to love songwriting for the sake of writing songs, not because of the accolades it might bring. If you write to get famous, you're putting too much value on the results and using your gift solely for personal reasons instead of using it to impact others. Everyone, no matter their level of visibility, is able to influence the lives of those around them. However, not everyone is going to be in the spotlight. If your main purpose in writing is the pursuit of fame, you are actually misusing your gift and you will eventually find yourself really frustrated and resenting those who have what you want.

While I'm a huge supporter of writing songs for personal expression and creative outlet, God didn't put us on earth to make a name for ourselves. Therefore, that shouldn't be our motivation. It's an empty pursuit and ultimately will never bring the satisfaction and fulfillment we're looking for. Those things come only from partnering with the Lord and His purposes for us. (Hint: It's all about impacting the lives of others.)

The book of Matthew says that out of the overflow of the heart, the mouth speaks. Meaning that what is in your heart will leak out. When your heart is in the wrong spot, your songs can become tainted by what's inside and will not carry the same poignancy and authority they would have otherwise. Or worse, they may even transfer the pain, disappointment or anger you are feeling to the listener, leaving them worse off than they were before they heard your song.

The reason I'm including this mini-sermon is that so much emphasis is placed on songwriting in the church these days. It's an incredible thing, but it often leads to songwriters and worship leaders becoming the modern-day rock stars within the church. It's very alluring, and it's far too easy to get swept up in the desire for fame instead of pointing people back to the Lord.

Write because you love to write. Write because it's in you to do it. Write to bring honor to God and to touch others through your gift. As you steward even the smallest opportunities He brings you, He will bring you more and will take you everywhere you need to go. I promise you that.

## WRITE LIKE YOU

The best song you can write is the one that is most authentically you. Being inspired by someone else is great. Learning from another's style and imitating it are both very natural. In reality, we are all products of our influencers. However, the more you write, the more you will begin to find your own voice and style. When you do, own it! God gave you a unique style, and you've experienced life in a way no other person has. Because of these things, you have something completely original to say and express. The most satisfying shoes to fill are your own because they were made just for you.

## LEAN ON MORE MATURE WRITERS

Everyone has to start somewhere. This includes the most famous songwriters you know. At one point, they were unknowns hammering out songs in their bedrooms just like the rest of us. What got them to where they are now? Hard work, for one. But they also learned from more seasoned writers one way or another.

One of the times I grew the most as a writer was when I sat down with Jeremy Riddle to show him an idea I was working on. He gave the song a good listen and then asked me a simple, straightforward question: "What do your verses have to do with your chorus?" I grinned sheepishly and admitted, "Absolutely nothing."

He went on to tell me my verses weren't bad, but they weren't all that unique either. The content was a bit generic, and it didn't really support the theme of the rest of the song. He was convinced I had more to say than what was on the page and encouraged me to rework my verses.

As much as I wanted him to say, "Great job! What a song! It's totally finished!" I knew he was right. So I went home, took his advice and worked. What came out of the rewrite was immensely better than what I had started with. What's more, the advice he gave me became a new standard for my writing, and the songs that came later benefited from the experience.

Find people who are better than you and learn from them. Even if their style isn't the same as yours, you'll still find things to learn. No one becomes an expert on their own.

Even if you don't have someone more experienced currently in your life, you can learn from established writers in other ways.

In the audio production world, there's something called "reverse engineering." A producer listens to a previously recorded song with the purpose of finding out how they did what they did. "How did they get that tone? What effects did they use to give it that vibe?" You can do this same thing with songwriting.

Study your favorite songs. What is it about those songs that stands out to you? Take note of the lyrics. Do they carry the theme throughout the song? What creative phrases stand out? What's another way you could say the same thing?

There are tons of things to be learned by listening with intention.

PART TWO

# DOING THE WORK

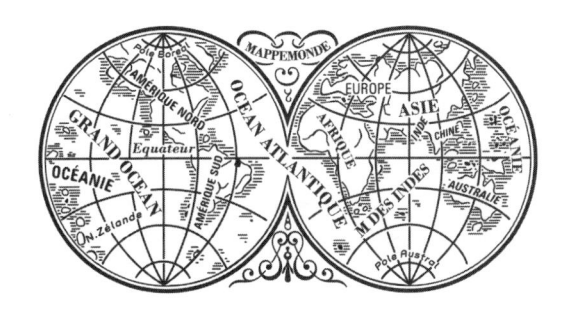

*"There are no shortcuts to any place worth going."*

Beverly Sills

# THE SONGWRITER'S ADVOCATE

## STARTING A SONG

"Where do I start? Is it better to write a melody first or lyrics? Do I need to know what I'm going to write before I start?"

Those are questions I get asked a lot, and they are great questions. You obviously have to start somewhere. Often it's just by showing up and trying.

Everyone's process is a little bit different and that's how it should be. But here's some simple advice: Start with what you get. I've found myself starting songs a number of ways, and they've all worked out.

To help you get going, here are some of the more common starting points.

## SOMETHING PREVIOUSLY WRITTEN OR CREATED

This is a very common one, especially in the church. We tend to center a great deal of songs around passages or concepts from the Bible, and the reason is obvious: because it's full of life. However, song ideas can come from many places. A simple poem. A moving art piece. A heartfelt moment in a movie. Even other songs. All are valid places to look if you know what it is you are seeking: something that moves your heart. That is where the best songs come from.

I know of some writers who actually write new lyrics to existing songs that inspire them. They take the same rhythms and melodies and use them as a launching pad for their own songs. Because the song already has a strong structure and flow, using it as a starting point can be really productive. It helps you focus on one thing at a time instead of multiple aspects simultaneously.

I realize this method may sound like "cheating" to some people, but in reality, there is nothing new under the sun. It's virtually impossible to write anything without being inspired by someone else's work. If you've watched many movies, you've no doubt noticed there's a pattern in the way the stories are told. Girl meets guy. Guy is a jerk and girl says, "I can't stand that guy!" Something happens, like a tragedy or heroic act, and girl sees guy in a new light. Girl and guy end up falling in love. End scene. I've just summarized about 90 percent of all romantic comedies out there. Why is it so many storytellers follow this pattern? Because it works and they know it.

When you write this way, you're using an existing blueprint to build your house. The location of the walls may be the same, but the paint colors, flooring, countertops, etc. will all be different. What makes the house yours are the choices you make after the walls are in place.

If you decide to try this approach, make sure you change up the melody and any lyrics that seem similar to the original before releasing the song.

## A RANDOM PHRASE OR CONCEPT

These sorts of ideas can come from anywhere. Sometimes you "hear" a phrase in your head that stands out to you. Other times you think up a simple concept that seems like it has potential to tell a good story.

"Wouldn't it be cool if there was a song about a man meeting his birth parents for the first time? What kind of emotions would he experience? I wonder how the parents would react."

"If all the things I've been worrying about were taken care of, how would I feel? How could I put those feelings into a song?"

Simple questions or thoughts like these are where a ton of songs start. Someone catches a vision for what a song could convey and finds a way to put it to melody and lyric.

Several times I've started a song by coming up with the title first. I once wrote a song called "See the Sea" that started with just the title. The phrase "see the sea" randomly popped into my head, and I thought, *That sounds like a great title for a song. What would that song be about?*

I ended up telling a story about an old man who had wanted to see the ocean his whole life but had never taken the trip. He waited so long that he lost his vision and had to experience the trip through the eyes of his son.

*Can you see the sea*
*Can you describe it to me*
*For these old eyes can't open wide enough*
*To see if it really touches the sky*
*Just like these old ears have heard*

*Can you see the sea*
*Is it as close as it seems to be*
*Now these old hands have held a dream or two*
*For longer than I pray yours will do*
*Oh, don't you wait like me*

*Part Two: Doing the Work*

*Can you see the sea*
*Can you taste the salt on the breeze*
*Now these old legs can't take another step*
*But this old soul can't bear one more regret*
*So please, Son, carry me*

*Place me on the shoreline*
*With my face toward the sun*
*Let the waves finally wash over these tired bones*

*Adventure is a young man's game*
*Too long I've let life get in the way*
*Now this old world must take its toll on me*
*But his rough hands could never touch the peace*
*That this old heart has found*

I list this as an example of what can become of an idea. What started as a simple phrase turned into a concept that eventually became one of my favorite songs I've ever written.

Pay attention to the phrases and thoughts that pop into your head. You never know when one of them could turn into a song.

## SPONTANEOUS SINGING

Spontaneous worship is becoming increasingly more common in the church. It's a beautiful thing because in the midst of corporate worship, the Presence becomes so tangible. You're connected to the very Spirit of Creativity Himself, who is so creative that He actually created creativity. How's that for a concept?

When you're connected to Him, you have access to the endless wealth of creativity that He is. Out of that partnership, truly anything is possible.

Both spontaneous and prophetic moments of worship can be incredibly powerful places to start songs. Don't lose these starts. If your church records worship sets, get a copy of the sets you sing on and listen back. If they aren't recorded, don't be afraid to pull out your phone (discreetly, of course) and start recording. Keeping track of your ideas is one of the best ways to steward your gift.

If you don't have a place where you lead worship, try singing spontaneously on your own or to instrumental music. Again, look for something that inspires you and moves your heart. Chances are it will inspire and move the hearts of others as well.

## PERSONAL EXPERIENCE

Personal experience is one of life's most powerful teachers. Because that's true, songs written from personal experience tend to be very impacting. In my opinion, they are the most powerful type of song.

The honesty and transparency required to write these songs draw the listeners in because they understand the emotions behind the words. When you are able to connect with your listeners this way, you can powerfully impact them and even shape their lives.

The lessons you've learned can help others in their own process. The breakthrough you've had in your life can inspire others to find hope in their hearts. The faithfulness of God you've seen reminds others that He will fight for them as well. What's even cooler is that Revelation 19:10 says the testimony of Jesus is the spirit of prophecy. This means that when you give a testimony of what Jesus has done in your life, you're actually prophesying that same breakthrough into the lives of others.

Later in this chapter, I'll talk about personal worship songs versus corporate worship songs in more depth, but know that your history with the Lord and the lessons you've learned can translate powerfully into either category.

## KEEPING TRACK OF IDEAS

Song ideas can come from anywhere at any time. They'll jump into your head when you least expect them. You'll lie down on your bed at night and hear a melody. You'll be parking your car at work and all of a sudden think of that perfect line you've been looking for. You can't predict when the ideas will come, but it's vital you do something about them when they show up.

I can't tell you how many song ideas I've lost because I didn't write them down or record them. Find a way to keep track of your ideas, even if they don't seem life changing at the moment. Pull out that notebook and write those lyrics down. Grab your phone and record that melody, even if it's 3:00 a.m. Not every idea is going to make the cut, but no idea that is forgotten will ever become a song.

## CREATING A STRONG THEME

Once you've found a place to start, you need to determine the direction you want to take your song thematically. Sometimes your theme unfolds as you keep writing; other times you catch sight of it from the get-go. The important thing is that once you know what your theme is, you stick to it.

Consistency should be your goal. A mistake I've seen a lot of songwriters make is not keeping a consistent theme throughout their songs. This is a problem because you want your listeners to know what your song is about. When you ping-pong around from topic to topic, you leave the listeners confused and wondering what just happened.

Have you ever been in a meeting or a class where someone stood up to ask a question, but instead they started rambling about something that didn't make any sense? You can feel everyone in the room thinking, *Get to your point! What are you even talking about anyway?* Having a song without direction feels the same way.

A great writer communicates intentionally. They don't haphazardly throw a bunch of words that rhyme together and call it a song. Somewhere in the process, they figure out the direction of their song and start taking care to craft and refine it accordingly.

Again, you don't necessarily need to know the theme before you start writing. Some songs twist and turn their way toward completion and that's totally fine. But what makes a song end up being great is the effort put toward ensuring the theme is consistent when it's finished.

Each section of a song has a specific function in revealing the theme to the listener. I'll explain how this works later in the book.

## FINDING SOMETHING UNIQUE TO SAY

This is what separates the men from the boys, as they say. The challenge with songwriting as a whole is trying to say something common in an original way. This is particularly true when it comes to worship songs. While God is unlimited, our ability to describe Him is not. This results in the same phrases, concepts and passages of Scripture being used over and over again by songwriters around the world.

Here's a great example. There are a thousand and one songs out there that use the phrase "God is good." While it's a very true statement about the Lord, it's not all that original of a phrase. To branch away from cliché, you need to get specific. Don't just say He's good. Answer the question *how* He is good. It's in the specificity that you begin to dig beneath the surface and find much fresher language.

This is where songwriting gets really fun and more challenging because it pushes you to write better. It's always easier to say the first thing that comes to your head, but that's not the best practice. Putting in the extra work is always rewarding, and you may just surprise yourself with the depth and originality that comes out of it.

## THEMES TO AVOID

Like many "rules" in songwriting, this one may be considered highly subjective. As previously stated, I'm a firm believer in self-expression, and that includes writing songs about pain and hard periods of life. It can actually be really therapeutic to be raw and open about what you're going through. And to be honest, songs that make me "feel" are some of my favorites. However, you need to be aware of where you leave the listener.

Music is a powerful art form. Perhaps the most powerful because it weaves both movement and melody with the art of poetry. That being the case, leading the listener down a road of depression and hopelessness can be detrimental since it stirs up those emotions. The heavier the content, the more important it is for the resolution to shine through.

This is critical when writing for corporate worship. Focusing on our downfalls or shortcomings glorifies the problem instead of the solution (the Lord). Phrases like "I'm a mess" or "my life is falling apart" or "I can never get things right" do the opposite of what worship songs are supposed to do. Worship should always take people's attention off themselves and their circumstances and direct them to the Lord.

If you feel it's necessary to talk about a problem or struggle, it always needs to come in the context of hope. When you write songs about God, you're teaching people what He's like and that's a heavy responsibility.

There are tons of theological implications to consider behind this, but I'll leave you with this thought: If God is true to His Word, then He will make all things work together for our good. That means there is hope for every situation, and that should be clear in every song you intend to be sung in worship.

## PERSONAL VS. CORPORATE SONGS

If you've spent much time in the modern worship circle, you've likely heard songs referred to as personal worship songs or corporate worship songs. The difference between them is simple, although labeling songs as one or the other can be a little trickier. It all depends on the content and whether or not it applies to the majority of the congregation or just a few.

For example, by using the line "You saved me from my addictions," a writer is limiting their song to just those who have dealt with that particular struggle. It may be true on a personal level, and that's great for a personal worship song. However, if the writer's goal is for that song to be sung corporately, they need to write that line differently. Instead, they could say, "You saved me from the darkness," which opens wide the door of relevance because He saved us all from some form of darkness. Make sense?

The more specific you get about details of your own life, the more likely you are to start limiting your audience. Even saying something down the road of "my pride blinded me" or "I didn't think I needed You" could start to limit the corporate appeal of your song. Those sorts of statements get pretty specific, and not everyone will be able to relate to them.

Emotions, especially negative ones, can also be culprits of taking a song out of the corporate vein. Describing the way you feel may be very applicable to you, but someone who feels something different may not connect to the statement and, therefore, the song as a whole. A song that says things like "I am overwhelmed but I trust You" may be a good song to sing when you're actually feeling overwhelmed, but you probably don't feel that way all the time. A listener who can't connect in that moment to the emotion being portrayed may have a hard time relating to the song.

If in doubt, getting an outside opinion is really helpful. Play the song for a couple of friends and ask them what they think of the lines you're curious about. If they feel like the song is relatable to them and to others, there's a good chance it's fine.

Next, avoid really "out there" and abstract statements. If you're having a difficult time deciding whether or not to keep that one line, maybe ask yourself, "Can I see my mom singing this?" While that might seem a bit silly, a huge percentage of people in the church are moms, and not many moms would want to sing something like, "My guts are on fire for You," no matter how deeply you may feel that yourself.

Please don't take away from this that I'm telling you not to be creative or to push the envelope. I'm not saying that at all. But like any artist, you must refine your work.

Think of your song like a sculpture. It requires time and effort to take a stone and shape it into a statue. After finishing one of his greatest sculptures, Michelangelo is credited with saying, "I saw the angel in the marble and carved until I set him free." Think of your song like that. Write until the song comes out. That means work. It means not always keeping the first thing you write down. It means changing something that works into something that works better. And then maybe doing it again. All things worth doing are worth doing well. Songwriting is no different.

There's one more lesson to pull from this analogy. Michelangelo started with a stone, not a finished statue. Some people, perfectionists especially, get frustrated when their first attempts look way more like stones than they do statues. Stones don't become statues immediately or by accident. We all start with a big piece of stone, but only those willing to see the statue inside of it end up with a finished work.

What's great about personal worship songs (and personal songs in general) is that you can relax this "rule" about abstract statements. You can get away with using that super cool lyric you've been hanging on to, and it won't throw the congregation for a loop. However, the most memorable songs are the ones that intermingle creativity and craftsmanship, regardless of their intended audience.

Chances are that most, if not all, of the big-hitting worship songs you can name off the top of your head are corporate songs. Take some time and study the way the writers crafted those songs to apply to churches across the board. See how they approach emotions, if they do. See what statements they've made about our humanity and how they shaped those statements to relate to everyone.

# PART THREE
# CRAFTING YOUR SONG

*"Genius is 1% talent and 99% hard work."*

Albert Einstein

## WRITING AND REWRITING

One of the most challenging and exciting parts of writing a song is taking it from the original idea and turning it into something wonderful. It does not happen by itself, and it does not always happen easily.

Anyone who has written a book will tell you they went through a number of drafts before the book was released. Each draft brings the book closer to what the author is envisioning. Writing a song should be looked at the same way. Rarely is a song done on the first "draft." It typically needs to be worked over and ironed out.

I've heard people say things like, "But God gave me this song!" While that may be the case, God gave Adam the earth and told him to subdue it. There are no substitutes to hard work if you want a great end result.

## CREATING CONSISTENCY IN YOUR SONG

As a songwriter, one of your goals should be to make your song memorable. You want people to be impacted by your song but also to remember it. Creating consistency is a huge part of that. Inconsistent songs are harder to learn and sing because the lack of structure can create confusion for the listener. Here are a few things to consider as you work to create consistency.

## RHYTHM AND METER

If you've ever taken a poetry class, no doubt you are familiar with the concept of writing to a meter. It is the pattern or lyrical rhythm established by the number of syllables used in a line or section. By keeping a consistent meter, you create a sense of predictability that people can grab on to. Why is this important? I'd say it's for the same reason that keeping a consistent theme is important. Inconsistency is hard to follow.

This is particularly important when you're writing corporate worship songs. In your typical corporate worship setting, you're going to have a grab bag of people with various levels of musicality. Some will be very musical but most will not be. By having inconsistent or difficult patterns in your song, you're making it difficult for the average person to follow along. The whole point of corporate worship is to find ways to get the entire congregation worshiping together. The easier your song is to follow, the easier it will be for people to sing.

Let's look at the well-known song "One Thing Remains." This song is a great example of good metrical symmetry. We'll start with the first verse. Pay attention to the number of syllables in each line. Count them out:

> *Higher than the mountains that I face*
> *Stronger than the power of the grave*
> *Constant in the trial and the change*
> *One thing remains*

Do you see the pattern? Nine syllables for the first three lines, four on the last line. You can feel the lyrical rhythm of the song without much effort at all. When you couple this with its consistent melody (we'll talk more about consistent melody in a moment), a listener is able to follow along pretty quickly, maybe even after hearing it just once.

After you've established your pattern, I highly recommend you stick with it as you move forward. If you write a second verse, mimic the pattern from the first. If you write a second or alternate chorus, make sure it sings like the first chorus. Consistent patterns make for memorable, singable songs.

There are times when you'll need to add an extra syllable here or there for the sake of the lyrical message or proper grammar. The second verse of "One Thing Remains" actually does this:

> *On and on and on and on it goes*
> *It overwhelms and satisfies my soul*
> *And I never ever have to be afraid*
> *One thing remains*

If you count out the syllables in each line, the pattern here is actually nine, ten, eleven and four, which is a little different than the first verse. However, if you listen to the way it's sung, you'll notice that it flows very naturally and doesn't feel crammed. They were able to do this because the rhythm established by the first verse is still recognizable in the second verse. Take a listen to it sometime and pay attention to the slight differences. Even though they added an extra syllable or two at the beginning of the second and third lines, they did so without compromising the verse rhythm. Because of that, it works. But if they had tried to fit several extra syllables in, it would've been necessary to forcibly cram them in at the beginning of the line or alter the rhythm completely, killing consistency in the process.

Similarly, too few syllables can also throw the pattern off. When you don't have enough syllables in place, you have to awkwardly stretch words out over long sections of the melody, and that can be just as awkward to sing.

Inconsistency in patterns is probably the most common mistake I see when working with newer songwriters. It takes time and effort to put what you want to say within the confines of the meter, but it is so satisfying when you do! This is one of the many disciplines that will make you a better songwriter. Leaving a raw and undeveloped idea in your song is the easy route, but the easy route has never made anyone an expert.

Again, I'm not saying don't be creative. We were born to create, and there will be songs that push the envelope. However, you can't sacrifice your audience for the sake of "being cool and different." There are ways to break the mold, and I strongly encourage you to do that. Just keep in mind that the further you branch out from consistent structure, the more difficult it will be to get the average person to follow.

If your primary audience is not the Sunday morning crowd, that relaxes things a bit. Meter still plays a huge part in other types of songs (just take a listen to any pop song), but you have the liberty to mix things up a lot more because corporate singing is not the aim. However, I would still strongly encourage you to stick closely to the meter regardless of your intended audience because of the strength it gives your song.

# MELODY

The next thing is melody. Who wants to sing a boring song? I'm sure we can all think of some songs on the radio and wonder how they got there, but those are going to be the exceptions and not the rules.

A good melody is the perfect blend of the expected and the unexpected. Your melody should sound new and familiar at the same time. You accomplish this primarily through creating basic repetition and then deviating from it. Let me explain what I mean.

When writing a song, you want the melodies of each section to feel distinct and discernible from the others. When you transition from your verse to your chorus, you want the listener to be able to tell. When your whole song has the same melody, everything runs together and gets boring pretty quickly. This is unwanted repetition, where all the sections of your song blur together to create a somewhat forgettable mess. Modifying chord progressions from section to section is an easy and important way to break things up, but making sure your melody varies is even more important.

Simple repetition *within* each section is a different story. That is the type of repetition you want. By repeating melodic patterns, you create a desirable predictability and familiarity in your song. This is very similar to what we talked about with rhythm and meter. By creating these patterns, you are giving your listeners something they can easily grab on to, making the song easier to learn and easier to get stuck in people's heads (which is always a great compliment to a writer).

As you are building your melody, try to create patterns that spread out and don't repeat themselves too quickly. What is too repetitive? Well, this can be a bit subjective, but if you have the same melody for every line of a section, it could end up getting old quickly. Try spreading your melodic pattern out over two lines before repeating it. Or perhaps change the last note or two every other line to give it some variation.

It really is a bit of a balancing act. Too much repetition too quickly and the melody gets old. Too little repetition and the melody has a hard time becoming familiar.

You can also think of your melody as a call and response. Musically speaking, a melody that ends on a high note (your melody goes up at the end) feels unresolved. It's sort of like asking a question but not letting it be answered. Or watching someone swing upward on a swing set only to stay suspended awkwardly in the air. It leaves the listener hanging and waiting for a resolution, which you should give them. Like the old adage says, what goes up must come down. If your melody climbs the scale for the first line, bring it back down for the next line. By doing this, you are providing a call and response, a question and an answer. It's very appealing to listeners, and it's a classic, time-tested songwriting technique.

These concepts may be a little difficult to convey in writing, but take a listen to some popular songs (worship or otherwise) and pay attention to where melodies repeat themselves and where and how they vary. You'll find that most of them have very easy patterns to sing, which is why they are so memorable.

## PRONOUNS

Another common mistake I see some writers make is switching pronouns and perspectives mid-song. Meaning that songs use *I, me* and *my* in one section and then *we, us* and *ours* in the next. Or *He, Him* or *His* become *You* and *Yours,* while still talking about the same person. While this is not a make-or-break rule (because there are some big songs out there that do it), it can create a little confusion, especially if it changes within the same section. It causes people to say, "Wait. Who am I singing about again?"

Remember, consistency is an important goal in everything we do as writers because it makes our songs stronger and easier to learn and remember. A good rule of thumb is if you start with one perspective, keep it consistent throughout the song unless you are clearly writing from the aspect of different people.

## THE FUNCTION OF EACH SECTION

A song has four basic parts: verse, chorus, bridge and (on occasion) pre-chorus. Each of these parts serves a function, both musically and lyrically. Having a good understanding of these functions will help give you direction as you write and create strong, memorable songs.

What I'm about to outline is what I would call a "soft" songwriting formula. It is not the only way to write a song, but it is one way and it works well. The strength of this formula is that it helps focus your theme with the intent of getting your song's message across to the listener.

Again, this book primarily focuses on writing for corporate worship, but many of the following principles will carry across into other categories of songs as well.

## THE FUNCTION OF YOUR CHORUS

I want to talk about the chorus first because it is possibly the most important part of your song. Yes, all parts of your song are important, but a strong chorus covers a multitude of decent verses and bridges. Have you ever noticed that when you ask someone how a song goes, they almost always sing the chorus? Why is that? It's because the chorus contains the central theme of your lyrics and the song's main musical hook. It should be the most memorable part of your song. This is the part of the song you want people to walk away singing after you've finished playing it.

Again using "One Thing Remains" as an example, you can see the central message of the song in the chorus:

> *Your love never fails*
> *It never gives up*
> *It never runs out on me*

What is the point of your song? Your chorus should answer that question. It is the "what" of the song. What's your song about? Well, listen to the chorus. Whatever theme you want your song to be about or whatever point you're trying to get across, it should be clearly evident here. The other sections should play support roles to your chorus.

This is also where that healthy melodic repetition comes in. You want the melody to have just enough predictability so your listener can sing it after hearing it only a few times. Again, you want it to be your main hook and the most interesting part of your song. The part the listener can't wait to get to. The place where the song lands and naturally seems to want to return to when given the opportunity.

## THE FUNCTION OF YOUR VERSE

Your verses should set up your chorus. Think of each verse as the "why" or "how" to the "what" of your song. If your chorus is about the goodness of God, for example, your verses should say *why* you believe He's good or *how* you know He's good. Similarly, if your chorus tells of God's faithfulness, your verses should describe the ways He's been faithful. By the time you reach your chorus, your theme should be clear because of the context you gave in your verses.

> *Higher than the mountains that I face*
> *Stronger than the power of the grave*
> *Constant through the trial and the change*
> *One thing remains*

What is that one thing? The chorus clearly answers that question: *Your love never fails.*

Many writers tend to abuse the meter the most here. Perhaps it's because they feel the bulk of their content needs to come in the verses, or maybe it's because narrowing down ideas is challenging. Whatever their reasoning, you want the picture you're painting to be detailed, yes, but also clear and precise.

If you're writing more than one verse, try to keep the flow consistent between them. The more recognizable the timing (meter) and melody from one verse to the next, the better.

There's something so very satisfying about saying exactly what you want to say while fitting it into the song's existing structure. That's what good songwriting is all about. Just remember, a clean meter helps your audience learn your song and sing along. The more erratic or complicated the meter gets, the more difficult the song will be for others to learn.

The melody for your verses should be interesting yet not quite as dynamic as that of your chorus. Your song should naturally lift from the verse (the set-up scene) to your chorus (the main act). You don't necessarily need your verses to be "hooky," so you can play with the melodic patterns a bit here. They don't need to be quite as tight as your chorus, but they should still be clean and strong. The call-and-response approach works really well in verses (one line creates musical tension that the next line resolves). You can have a lot of fun with verses. Try stretching the patterns out to be longer, perhaps over multiples lines. Or maybe vary them a bit instead of using the same call and response over and over.

## THE FUNCTION OF YOUR PRE-CHORUS

I have only a few thoughts on writing pre-choruses. In essence, they are transition sections and function to seam the verse and chorus together. While they do serve a purpose, most songs don't actually need them. In fact, I have never written a pre-chorus on purpose. However, it doesn't mean that a songwriter can't, or shouldn't, use them.

In my opinion, the only time a pre-chorus is actually necessary is when you have a musical or lyrical gap you can't fix any other way. In other words, if your verse feels like an incomplete thought thematically, or it seems musically awkward transitioning to the chorus, a pre-chorus might fix your problem.

The best way to determine whether your song needs the pre-chorus you've written is to ask yourself, "Does this create more clarity for my theme, or is it just more content?" In many cases, adding additional content doesn't actually add to the song. Sometimes more is just more. There's nothing wrong with simplicity as long as you're getting your message across.

Melodically, you should craft your pre-chorus to lift you up to the chorus. It should be like running up a flight of stairs to the main landing with a dramatic, "Ta-da!" Most pre-choruses create musical tension (the call) that is resolved by the chorus (the response).

*Part Three: Crafting Your Song*

## THE FUNCTION OF YOUR BRIDGE

When it comes to writing your bridge, think of it as the "because" of your theme. Your chorus communicates a truth (the "what") that is backed up by your verses (the "why" or "how"), which then naturally leads to some kind of result (the "because").

In my opinion, there are two main types of bridges in worship songs, both of which function as the "because": the response and the declaration. Depending on your song's message and theme, you may find one of these two bridges more appropriate than the other.

In a response bridge, you're giving the congregation an opportunity to respond to the Lord in a way that relates to the song's theme. For example, if your theme is about the goodness of God, you could respond with thanks in the bridge. *Because* of His goodness, you want to respond. Or if your theme focuses on the Lord's sovereignty, you could respond with surrender. Make sense? A response bridge can be incredibly powerful because it brings your listener to a point where they are no longer just singing a song, but they are actually interacting with the Lord.

A declaration bridge is exactly what it sounds like: declaring something about yourself or about the Lord. The purpose of a declaration is to leave people with something to take away with them from the worship experience.

Making declarations is a great way to remind ourselves of what's important. They remind us of who God is. That He's fighting on our behalf. That He's always working all things out for our good. They remind us of who we are. That we are children of God. That we are more than conquerors. They remind us of what the Lord has done. That He made a way for us. That we don't have to earn His love. Because of what the Lord has done, here are truths we can declare.

The bridge of "One Thing Remains" is a declaration bridge.

*In death in life I'm confident and*
*Covered by the power of Your great love*
*My debt is paid there's nothing that*
*Can separate my heart from Your great love*

Remember, your song is an encounter waiting to happen. Your goal should be to bring people to a point where they can interact with the Lord and walk away changed. A well-thought-out bridge can help facilitate this interaction by driving home the purpose and message of your song.

Musically speaking, your bridge should do one of two things: launch or land. This is primarily determined by the "feel" of your song.

If your song is fast and punchy, it probably could use a musical break. Bringing it down to a simple, less dynamic bridge will be a breath of fresh air in the midst of all the energy. With a "down" bridge like this, treat the melody like you would a pre-chorus and build it up at the end to lift it back into the chorus.

If your song is more on the mellow side, a big, bold bridge could be a great fit. You can treat the bridge's melody a little more like a second chorus but one that lifts up from the chorus (musically and melodically), so it can drop back to the chorus at the end. This kind of bridge should be the most dynamic part of your song, so don't be afraid to build it up and make it count.

Again, this is not the only way to write a song, but it does work well. I've also heard of people approaching a song like a math problem. PROBLEM + SOLUTION = RESULTS. Describe a problem in your verses, add the solution in your chorus and then explain the solution's results in your bridge. "I was a prisoner" + "You came and saved me" = "now I'm free." There really are many ways to write a great song.

As I said earlier, building and maintaining a theme is tremendously important to your song because it sets it up to impact the listener. A song without direction is a song lacking in purpose. My hope is that as you grasp the concepts outlined in this section, it will help you hone your themes and bring life and purpose to your songs.

## A CASE FOR CO-WRITING

Co-writing is one of the best things a songwriter can do, particularly when it comes to finishing a song. Some of the best songs in the world are co-writes. Pick a handful of your favorite songs and look at the songwriting credits. I can guarantee that tons of them will have multiple writers. Co-writing can make your songs stronger.

When you bring in another writer, you bring in a fresh perspective and a fresh set of ideas that can spark your own imagination and creativity.

When I was a younger songwriter, I had a hard time with co-writing. I felt like I had something to prove, so I had to finish every song I started myself. I couldn't ask for help because if I did, it would mean I wasn't a good enough writer to finish a song on my own. It was really exhausting. But one day, the Lord stopped me in the middle of my striving and told me that songs are encounters waiting to happen. He said that my unwillingness to let people help me would keep songs from being finished. If that happened, it meant the encounters people were supposed to have with Him through those songs would never happen.

It was a little sobering and, needless to say, I changed my tune on co-writing pretty quickly. When you write a worship song, you are setting people up to experience God in powerful, life-changing ways. That's something to take very seriously, and co-writing is just one of the many ways to steward that responsibility.

## CO-WRITING: SIFTING THROUGH IDEAS

You don't have to keep every idea someone gives you. A good rule of thumb is if you started the song, it's your song. That means you are not obligated to use every idea given to you in the process. Not every idea is going to be good, and even good ideas may not fit the direction you envisioned as the initial innovator. If you have any concerns about hurting someone else's feelings, feel free to discuss your intentions up front. The more communicating you can do before you write, the more potential messes you'll avoid.

## CO-WRITING: BE OPEN MINDED

Don't be so married to your song that you turn down good ideas. A friend of mine tells a story about the first time he sat down with an acclaimed worship writer. He had what he considered to be a great song and was excited to show it to the other writer. The other writer, however, had several suggestions for the song. Change this line here. Say this word instead. This part doesn't work, so do this instead. It was a hard thing for my friend to hear, since he was a younger writer and was really happy with the way the song already was. However, the feedback was beneficial and the song became a massive hit. Would it have still been a hit without the extra feedback? Possibly, but the song became stronger because of the input of others.

## CO-WRITING: CREDIT WHERE CREDIT IS DUE

Establish percentages and splits before you start writing. This means figure out a system to give credit where credit is due. This is massively important, and I can tell you horror stories about how messy things can get when this sort of communication doesn't happen up front. There are several ways to approach this and they can all work, so long as the terms are agreed upon in advance.

One of the more standard ways to determine splits is to decide which parts of the song are the most important. When it comes to modern music, chorus is king. It is the main hook of the song, and it gets sung the most. This means it is the "most important" part of the song, and as such, it is worth the most percentage.

After the chorus, the bridge is probably the next biggest part of the song. It is almost as important as the chorus, but since it's not the main hook, it holds a little less value. From there, verses and pre-choruses probably land about equal. They are key parts of the song but don't get as much play time as the chorus. They usually get sung once, maybe twice, each time the song is done.

Here's an example of what the percentages could look like:

*Chorus = 40%*
*Bridge = 30%*
*Verse 1 = 15%*
*Verse 2 = 15%*

In the event that you have a song with a pre-chorus, simply adjust the percentages to accommodate it.

Like many aspects of songwriting, how to break up percentages is subjective. Some may argue that verses are just as important as the chorus because of how they provide context the chorus wouldn't have without them. Or maybe they think a song is worthless without a chorus, so it should be worth way more than other sections. The percentages you pick aren't really the issue—it's making sure people know what to expect before you write that's important.

How do you account for melody? Well, the same basic idea can apply to melodies, too. What's a song without a melody, anyway? It's a rap, I guess, and if that's the case, you probably don't need to worry about this part.

What's more important to a song: the lyrics or the melody? Since you can't really have one without the other (raps and instrumentals aside), I'd say they're equally important. That means they need to have equal value: 50 percent lyrics, 50 percent melody.

If you wrote just the lyrics or just the melody for a section, you should get half the credit for that section. If you wrote both, you should get all the credit. Right? Right.

Another way people distribute credit is by splitting a song evenly between everyone involved in the process. In other words, if you were in the room, you get a piece. While this is a very kind approach, it's not always practical. If Joe is in the corner on his phone and not really contributing to the process, most people would agree he probably doesn't deserve songwriting credit because he didn't actually write any songs. However, this model works well for a lot of writers, and if you make a point not to write with people like Joe, it could work great for you as well.

## CO-WRITING: WHEN NOT TO GIVE CREDIT

Let's talk about when you do not need to give songwriting credit. Obviously, if someone has written lines or sections for your song or helped you with large, transformative changes ("Bob, your verse is a chorus"), they should be given credit for their contribution to the final product. But there are certain situations in which you don't need to give credit to another writer.

Like I said previously, if you started the song, it's your song. That means people will make suggestions or write parts you may not want to keep for the final product. If a section someone else wrote does not make the cut, there is no real reason to give them a percentage. Besides, just because a section didn't make the song it was originally written for doesn't mean it can't fit into another song. They can hang on to it and use it later. That happens all the time. I have innumerable song fragments and ideas I'm holding on to until they find a home.

Similarly, you do not need to give credit for changes to the chord progression. I'll revisit this later in the book, but chord progressions are not copyrightable. Because of this, they are not recognized as "intellectual property" (a fancy phrase that means "something you created through artistic endeavors"). So this means if someone changes your chord progression, legally they would have no claim to your song.

The last thing you may not need to give credit for is small and insignificant changes. There have been times when I've suggested a very small change to a friend's song, and I did not ask for or expect songwriting credit. These sorts of changes, like changing a single word or note, are very minor tweaks and are more like giving advice than actually writing a song.

You might ask, "But didn't you help them finish their song?" Yes, I did, but I considered my "contribution" to be very minor. With the group of writers I worked with at the time, that was the understanding we had. It worked and we all agreed to it.

In an instance where a single word changes the entire dynamic of a song, or perhaps becomes the core or central word for the song, I would not consider that "minor." How much was the song altered by that one change? That's the question to answer.

Not everyone may like the approach I outlined above, which is fine. What's most important is to know what the other writers are thinking. It is also important to know that you can do whatever feels best to you. If you want to give someone credit for even the most minuscule contributions, it's totally up to you. Heck, I've given songwriter credit to someone for helping me structure and define a song, even though they did very little actual writing on it. I'm presenting these ideas as basic guidelines to give you a starting point for making decisions, not as a hard and fast rule everyone needs to follow.

## HOW TO APPROACH CO-WRITING

How on earth *do* you co-write? What's the best format? Well, every writer is different, so it's important to know how you are the most comfortable and the most productive. That will be the best format for you.

There are two main ways to co-write: working on an idea in a room together or working on things separately and sending ideas back and forth through one means or another. Both can be effective, and neither one is more right than the other.

When writing together in the same room, I recommend having a place to start. If you sit down with another writer and neither of you has any ideas, chances are your songwriting session will be short. Bring an idea to the table, even if it's a single line. It will give you something to work toward and will help the productivity of the songwriting session.

It can be uncomfortable for some writers to throw out ideas in front of other people. If that's you, you may find that working on co-writes solo feels less vulnerable. But understand that the more you sit down and write with others, the easier it gets.

If you prefer to work on co-writes alone or need to because of distance, find a good way to keep track of your progress. It's probably a good idea to save the voice memos or audio files you've been sending each other and make sure you date them. This way, if anything needs to be cleared up or referred to later, you have an unmistakable record of your progress.

Again, keep an open mind in this process and learn to develop thick skin. Writing with other people does require a level of vulnerability, but it is very rewarding.

*Part Three: Crafting Your Song*

## WORK FOR HIRE VS. SONGWRITING ROYALTIES

With the rise of digital recordings, getting music recorded and out there has become exponentially easier. As a result, it's increasingly more common for churches, even ones with limited budgets, to record and release albums. Many churches (and some labels) take two primary approaches when writing for albums, and I want to break them down for you quickly, in case you ever find yourself in this scenario.

The first is the traditional approach of writing for songwriting credit (as I described in the last section). Once the song is written, splits are determined, and the songwriters get paid their cut for as long as the album sells or the song is played.

Keeping track of song splits can take a fair amount of administration, so sometimes people may want to take the easier approach of hiring writers to write for an album. As no splits are required, there is a lot less to keep track of. The writers are hired to write, and once the project is done, they get paid and are on their way.

If you are approached about working for a project like this, it's important to know what you're getting into.

When you are hired to create, you typically do not own the rights to what you just created. You were compensated for your creative efforts, and that's all you get. If a song happens to blow up or the album does well, everything is owned by whoever hired you to do the writing, and you probably won't get paid anything else. An obvious downside. On the other hand, even if the album tanks, you've already been paid. You walk away with money in your pocket regardless.

Both approaches have clear pros and cons. Both can work well and either one can let you down, but I thought it best to discuss them for the sake of education, if nothing else. Forewarned is forearmed and all that.

PART FOUR

# FINISHING THE SONG

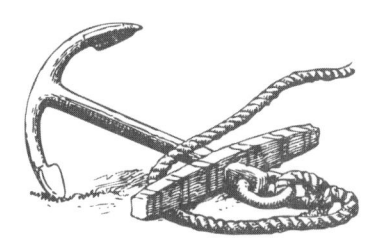

"*The writer's secret is not inspiration—for it is never clear where it comes from—it is his stubbornnes, his patience.*"

Orhan Pamuk

## APPROACHING THE FINISH LINE

When your song is nearing completion, there are several things you need to start thinking about. How do you know when your song is finished? And once it is finished, do you need to copyright your songs? What about publishing? Are there ways you can make a little money off of this? All very good questions. To see the process through to its end, there are several important (and some rather technical) things you should consider.

## HOW TO KNOW YOUR SONG IS FINISHED

After you've been working and working on a song, how do you know when it's finished? Like so many other aspects of artistic expression, it can be difficult to say. What is finished to one writer may not be finished to the next. It really is a tricky subject to master.

In reality, some songs may never feel finished to you. Several years back, I was writing a song for a project, and the deadline was fast approaching. I spent several days trying to shape the song into what I had in my head. I even sat down with a couple of other writers to get ideas to help me finish, but nothing quite landed. Eventually, the deadline arrived and the higher-ups told me they were happy with where the song was, and off it went to the studio. To be honest, I wasn't completely satisfied with the song yet, but a deadline is a deadline and I had to accept that.

There is a point in the process where you've given it your all, and you simply don't have the creative capacity to bring it the rest of the way. If you find yourself in this situation, this is a great time to bring in a co-writer. A fresh set of eyes and ideas is often just the spark needed to get the fire going again to see that song through to completion.

Other times, you may just need to tuck that song in your back pocket and move on to other songs. You'll bog yourself down if you pour all your energy into a song you're stuck on. You can always come back to it later. In the meantime, you could be writing brand new material if you only had the time and energy available for it. Some songs have taken me years to finish. The important thing is that you continue to write and not give up on your songs, even if you have to press pause on them for a time.

## THE TESTING PHASE

Typically, I have a pretty good idea of when a song is at least close to being done. I've studied my lyrics to make sure my theme is clear and supported throughout the song. I've made sure the melody and meter are consistent, and I've tweaked any sections that are off. I've done my best to fix any of those lingering lines I wasn't completely happy with. And overall I feel like I've communicated my thoughts effectively. At this point, I'm ready to start testing the song out. This is really important, especially if you aren't completely happy with where the song is. Maybe it's close but not quite "there" yet.

There are a couple of things you can try to help you determine if a song is solid enough to be called "done." These are not foolproof, but they are very practical steps that should prove helpful.

The first step is to play your song for someone. It's actually really helpful not only to sit down with other songwriters but also with people who just love music. Ask them if they can identify your theme. Ask them if they feel like that theme is consistent throughout the song or if any parts feel off or random to them. Take any feedback they give you, and test it out on your song. Even if you don't end up keeping the changes, trying things out helps you stay humble and sharpens your writing skills.

The next step is to try it live. This is a really powerful test for a worship song because you get to see what happens with it in a corporate setting. How does the room feel when you're singing? Does the congregation respond to the song initially? Do they respond at all? Are there sections of the song that feel like they lose momentum, or does it stay on track the whole time?

I would definitely recommend recording the song when you're trying it out. Even if it's just somebody's phone at the soundboard, having some kind of reference to go back to after the fact is always helpful. There have been times when I thought a song fell flat from the stage, but it felt completely different when I watched or listened to the set later.

It's also important to remember that brand new songs may take a couple of times to catch on with a congregation. They're hearing it for the first time, so they may need time to learn it before they grab onto it.

Don't make assumptions too quickly if it doesn't go over the first time. If things don't fly the way you hoped, that's okay. Take the song back to the workshop and do a little more ironing and refining.

## COPYWRITING

Once you've decided your song is done, you should think about getting it copyrighted.

This is the part of songwriting that loses a ton of people. It's a bit tedious and more than a little overwhelming, especially when you first start looking into it. Regardless of how confusing the process may seem, protecting your work is worth it, which is where copyrighting comes in.

*Note: This process is a little different from country to country, so if you live outside of the U.S., make sure you familiarize yourself with your country's copyright laws and procedures.*

When you first write your song, it is technically copyrighted on the grounds that you have created something that is your personal intellectual property. As soon as it is in a fixed format (i.e., lyrics on a page, recording in your phone, etc.), you own it. While this does give you some level of security, it may or may not be enough to help you in court if someone steals any of your content.

You may have heard of "the poor man's copyright," which is when you mail a copy of your song, in some format, to yourself and leave it unopened. Because it is stamped and dated by a government agency (the postal service), some believe this can give you more security in a government-run court than having nothing at all. However, there is some debate over whether or not this will be sufficient evidence in court, so I don't recommend this method.

As they say, nothing beats the real thing. The Copyright Office exists for the sole purpose of protecting you and your work. If you have your song copyrighted, you are in the best position possible. If you are going to record, release or publicly perform your song, registering it properly is the absolute best practice.

Before I get into how you do this, it's very important to know the difference between a composition and a sound recording, especially if you intend to record your song.

The composition is the heart and soul of your song: the lyrics and melodies. It is what you created and it can be legally copyrighted.

A sound recording refers to an arrangement of your composition that has been recorded. It consists of things like chord progressions, arrangements and stylization. A composition can be copyrighted, but a chord progression cannot be. Why is this important? For one, when you hire a producer, they will most likely make changes to things like chord progressions, tempos and arrangements. That's why you hire them in the first place—to bring structure and style to your song. Unless they make changes to your melody or lyrics, they do not own any rights to the song itself.

Another reason to know the difference between a composition and a sound recording is to ensure you copyright your song the correct way. You want to make sure you are protecting each composition. To do that, you need to copyright each song as an individual "work" (as it is called by the Copyright Office). You will be given the option to copyright a sound recording, but that will not protect the lyrical and melodic content of your song.

Copyrighting is actually not that complicated, once the mystery is taken out of it. Once you're ready to move forward, all you really need to do is follow these steps:

1. Make a recording of your song. It doesn't need to be fancy, but it needs to be clear enough to hear your lyrics and melodies.
2. Create a profile on copyright.gov. This takes less than two minutes.
3. Register a new "work of the performing arts" (again, this is a composition, not a sound recording) and supply all needed information. This part of the process can be a little confusing, so make sure you take your time and read through things carefully.
4. Pay the applicable fee.
5. Upload your recording.

It can take several months to hear back from the Copyright Office, so don't sweat if you don't get a response right away. You could also do this whole process by mail, but it does add to the waiting period.

## PUBLISHING

While not as vital as copyrighting, getting a publishing deal can be very beneficial. Essentially, a publisher is a person or company that comes alongside you and helps to promote your song in hopes of getting it covered by other artists, placed on films, radio and television ads, etc. More exposure for your song means more possibilities for income. A publisher also ensures your song is copyrighted and registered in all the right places, and they will handle any licensing requests that come in (meaning when someone wants to record your song, your publisher makes sure you get paid for it). In essence, a publisher is there to promote, protect and collect on your song.

There are a few aspects to having a publisher you should be aware of. First off, publishers do not do all of this for free. When you sign a traditional publishing deal, you are actually giving the publishing company partial ownership of your song (industry standard is roughly a 50 percent split). You lose profits, yes, but a good publisher can help your song go much further than it would have on its own.

Another thing to consider is that publishers typically work with tons of artists. That means tons of songs for them to sift through, and tons of songs that might slip through the cracks. You aren't guaranteed any kind of placement, nor are you ensured all your songs will get promoted.

Finally, getting a publishing deal can be difficult. The more prestigious the publishing company, the harder it is to land a deal with them. They won't want to promote songs they don't consider to be worth their while. Unless you've made some sort of name for yourself, you might have a hard time getting the attention of "the big boys."

Like many other things, publishing deals have their pros and cons, and you'll need to make the best decision you can if given the opportunity. It is always advantageous to seek legal advice on a contract before signing.

There are other options to traditional publishing, however.

The first option is being your own publisher. You are technically your own publisher as soon as you write your song. You are able to promote, protect and collect on your song on your own and as you see fit. As your own publisher, you are not splitting ownership of your song with anyone, so any royalties that come in go straight to your pocket. However, you will need to ensure your song is registered in all the right places yourself so those royalties can actually find their way to you (more on that shortly). Any license requests that come in you'll need to issue and manage yourself.

The other option to consider is hiring a publishing administrator. A publishing admin handles all the "busy work" of publishing without taking ownership of your song. For a fee or small commission, they will make sure your songs are registered in the right places, will handle license requests and will make sure you receive what you are owed. This is a great option for people who don't want to mess with details but still want to get paid . . . which is everyone, right? Some of these companies, like TuneCore and CD Baby, can also help you distribute your music to digital music stores, satellite radio and streaming services. Just make sure you read up on what these companies will and will not do for your song if you hire them.

## WHERE SONGS SHOULD BE REGISTERED

Once your song is released, it should be registered in several places. This information primarily applies to writers who are self-publishing, but it is important for all writers to know so they can ensure their songs are being registered correctly by their publishers or admins.

*PROs*

Start by registering with a PRO (performing rights organization): ASCAP, BMI or SESAC. Whenever a song is played publicly via radio, TV, commercials, etc., payment is required. The PRO you register with will monitor when your songs are being performed and where, and they will make sure the rights have been purchased and you get your cut.

It's important to note that if you do not have a publisher or publishing admin, it's really smart to register as a publisher with the PRO as well. As PROs collect royalties, they split them up and designate 50 percent for the artist and 50 percent for the publisher. If you do not have a publisher to collect those funds, that 50 percent will never find its way to you.

*SoundExchange*

SoundExchange is very similar to a PRO except it primarily applies to non-interactive digital transmissions, like satellite and internet radio. Pandora is a great example of this. If your songs are distributed via these sources, income is being generated from the use of your music, which means funds are owed you. I highly recommend you register your songs with SoundExchange as well as with a PRO because PROs do not collect from these sources.

*CCLI*

CCLI is a licensing company specifically for lyrics displayed publicly in churches (like on the overheads during worship). If you are releasing worship songs, registering here is a must. As funny as it may sound, churches legally need to pay rights when they display your lyrics in a service. They do this by reporting to CCLI which songs they display each week. As this occurs, the membership fee churches pay is divvied up and sent to the owners of the songs. Even if you are the only person leading your song, there is still money to collect.

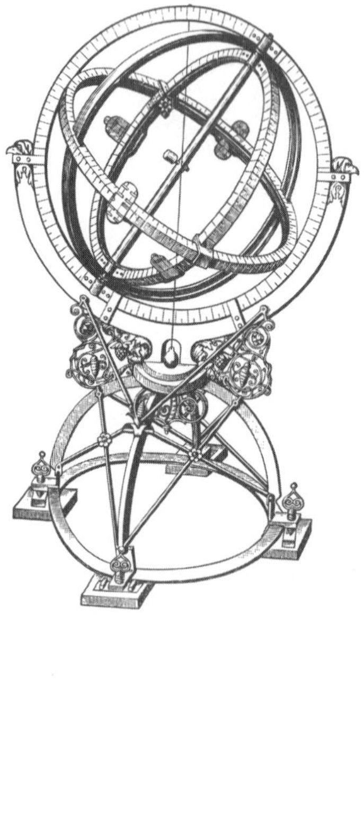

# FINAL THOUGHTS

One of the most challenging things I've been told as a songwriter was a charge Bill Johnson gave a group of us several years back. He said, "Write songs today about what you want the church to look like in five years."

As songwriters, we are influencers. All art forms are moving, but when you couple lyric and melody, something powerful happens. Music has the ability to shape lives and influence change, especially when we catch something the Lord is saying and put it to song. When we do, we are partnering with what the Lord is doing and, as Romans puts it, calling those things that are not as though they were.

My hope is that this book not only helps you become a better songwriter, but it also helps you realize how your songs can change those around you.

All throughout the Bible, you see people given favor and power from the Lord, but 100 percent of the time it's not just for their benefit. It's always for those around them. Samson was given great strength to defeat the Philistines. Solomon, who was given great wealth and wisdom, led a nation and was charged with building the temple where the Spirit of God would rest. Jesus had more favor than anyone else ever had or will have, and He used it to reach the outcasts of society. To heal the sick and raise the dead and ultimately change the direction of the world forever. In addition to all of that, He told His twelve closest companions that compared to all the miracles He did, they would do even greater things.

Your gift is important and so very needed, but never forget that it's not for your enjoyment alone. You are called to be a life changer. The more you steward your gift, the more you spend time crafting and refining your songs, the more impact those songs will have on the lives around you. And that, my friends, is why we write.

*Grace to you on your journey.*